COMMON SENSE

FOR

SAVING AMERICA'S

DEMOCRACY

ADDRESSED TO THE

CITIZENS

OF

THE UNITED STATES

of AMERICA

WRITTEN BY AN

AMERICAN

2024

THOMAS GRAHAM JR.

On the following interesting

S U B J E C T S

INTRODUCTION

THE VIEWS SET FORTH in this book in this divided age may not be of general acceptance. Great wrongs or inexcusable behavior or deeply false interpretation, if maintained for a lengthy period, will begin to become part of the established code of behavior of civilized man. Then a great reformer appears on the scene and points out how wrong or evil or false or untrue all of this is, and people will begin to change. Slavery in the eighteenth and nineteenth centuries is certainly an example. Individual elements of the moral code, such as the death penalty or individual behavior once thought to be worthy and strong, can over time come to be seen as onerous or destructive or even evil and intolerable. It happened to Senator Joe McCarthy of Wisconsin who, once thought to be a defender of our country's national security, later came to be seen as a scourge for the freedom of thought. He eventually drank himself to death.

These are difficult times for democracy in the United States some 248 years after the Declaration of Independence. The 2024 nominee of one of our nation's two great political parties, the Republican Party, which was once led by our greatest president, Abraham Lincoln, has indicated that he no longer cares anymore about our Constitution and intends if elected not to observe it in any way. Donald J. Trump, the nominee, previously (2017-2021) President of the United States of America, once publicly rebuked our excellent intelligence establishment for stating the obvious—that the dictator/president of Russia, Vladimir Putin, interfered with our presidential election in 2016—with Putin sitting right next to him, and the world public in front of him listening in via television. The president is supposed to be the servant and protector of this great country, but Trump acts as though he works not for his and our country but actually for one of the most evil and murderous leaders in the world, Vladimir Putin. Trump is subservient to the line coming from Moscow, and he is now trying to spread it among the free-thinking American people. He has perhaps a quarter of the people in the country blindly following him—the 25 percent—free American people following a president in thrall to a corrupt, criminal Russian ruler and himself, Donald Trump, a criminal and corrupt as well.

Fortunately, he was ousted from rule in 2020 by a man, Joseph Biden, a true American, a faithful follower of the Constitution and Bill of Rights. Biden has done an outstanding job as the president in both foreign and domestic policy. One of the best ever. However, he chose not to seek reelection.

Unfortunately, Trump is back on the scene, carrying initially 91 felony counts—indictments by our legal system of serious wrongdoings. Thirty-four of those are now discharged by conviction on all 34 in a jury trial in New York. Even so, the 25 percent who support Trump are still there. Many are people who object to immigrants from ethnic groups other than Northern Europeans and want to block such individuals from entering the country. The same sentiments apply to American citizens of color or alien ethnic groups that are not Northern European. They have a right to stay in the country but can never be more than second-class citizens. Trump tells the 25 percent that is what he will deliver, knowing himself that it is wrong and deeply un-American as well as impossible. George Washington, our first president and the commander of our victorious army of the Revolution, said as much at the successful end of the Revolutionary War in his farewell speech to his troops: "The bosom of America is open to receive not only the opulent and respectable stranger, but the oppressed and persecuted of all nations and religions . . ."

As far as Trump goes, one of our most influential, reputable, and heroic Founders, Alexander Hamilton, in effect, called him out in 1787:

> "A dangerous ambition more often lurks behind the specious mask of zeal for the rights of the people than under the forbidding appearance of zeal for the firmness and efficiency of government. History will teach us that the former has been found a much more certain road to the introduction of despotism than the latter, and that of those men who have overturned the liberties of republics, the greatest number have begun their career by paying an obsequious court to the people; commencing demagogues and ending tyrants."

As Liz Cheney, a former congresswoman and leader of the people, put it on the *NBC Today Show* on December 11, 2023, if Donald Trump is elected to a second term, he will not follow the Constitution, he will not allow another vote for president at the end of that term, he will never leave office, he will establish a dictatorship; in short, he will destroy our democratic republic. This is a very dangerous time; the choice in November of 2024 would be between the Constitution and a dictatorship. If Trump wins the vote in November, it could be the end of our democratic republic. On this point, my revered predecessor, Thomas Paine, though it was almost 250 years ago, gave the correct response to Liz Cheney:

> "The cause of America is in a great measure the cause of all mankind . . . [it] is the concern of every man [or woman] to whom nature has given the power of feeling; of which class, regardless of party censure, is the author."

> We all must ensure, as Abraham Lincoln stated in his Gettysburg Address, ". . . this nation, under God . . . and that government of the people, by the people, for the people, shall not perish from the earth."

Washington, DC
August 5, 2024

CHAPTER 1

THE MAN WHO WOULD BE KING

AMERICA ESCAPED from the role of colony and vassal of Great Britain in part by pursuing principles and objectives presented by my predecessor, Thomas Paine. These were set forth in *Common Sense*, published January 10, 1776, and made explicit in the Declaration of Independence dated July 4, 1776:

> "We, therefore, the Representatives of the united States of America, in General Congress, Assembled . . . solemnly publish and declare, That these United Colonies are, and of Right ought to be Free and Independent States; that they are Absolved from all Allegiance to the British Crown . . ."

On June 7, 1774, Richard Henry Lee had introduced a resolution in Congress (the Continental Congress, in existence since 1774) declaring "That these United Colonies are, and of right ought to be, free and independent States." Thomas Jefferson of Virginia was asked to write a draft declaration. This draft, when completed, was debated in the Continental Congress, and the Declaration was adopted on July 4, 1776. In it, the author made clear that in connection with independence,

> "We hold these truths to be self-evident, that all men [and women] are created equal, that they are endowed by their Creator with certain unalienable Rights, that among these are Life, Liberty and the pursuit of Happiness.--That to secure these rights, Governments are instituted among Men, deriving their just powers from the consent of the governed."

After a successful conclusion, in 1781, of the war for independence by the Continental Army, led by General George Washington, a peace agreement was concluded with Great Britain in 1783.

After an interim period of a few years, the 13 former colonies, now independent states, gathered together in Philadelphia and their people, through their representatives in Philadelphia, drafted a constitution to establish a set of laws and principles to govern this new state that the people were founding, the United States of America. It would have a president to lead it, not a king, and all rights of hereditary government that might exist were abolished and none could be established in the future. Indeed, no provisions for ennoblement of any kind could exist in this new state. Rights based on heredity were prohibited in this new republic. This was to be, as was said later by President Abraham Lincoln, that this was a country with a government "of the people, by the people, and for the people." The beginning lines of the Constitution are as follows:

> "We the People of the United States, in Order to form a more perfect Union, establish Justice, insure domestic

Tranquility, provide for the common defense, promote the general Welfare, and secure the Blessings of Liberty to ourselves and our Posterity, do ordain and establish this Constitution for the United States of America."

It is important to remember that all citizens, all state and federal officials, swear allegiance not ever to any man or woman but only to the Constitution. That and a commitment to the principles of the Declaration of Independence are the only two things that are required to be an American. Thus, there is not nor will there ever be any ethnic, geographical, racial, financial, or religious requirement to be an American.

The Declaration of Independence was written during the Age of Enlightenment in the eighteenth century. Certainly, it was influenced by the Enlightenment philosophers, such as John Locke, Jean Jacques Rousseau, and Montesquieu, and, undoubtedly, they supported its objectives, but there were two distinct intellectual influences who were most significant in shaping the form of the Declaration: Thomas Jefferson, its author and third president of the United States, and Thomas Paine, the author of *Common Sense*, the views and principles of whom played a major role in both the American and French Revolutions. This small book seeks to present a *Common Sense* for the twenty-first century, keeping in mind Hamilton's view as set forth in the introduction of the *Federalist Papers No. 1*: ". . . of those men who have overturned the liberties of republics, the greatest number have begun their career by paying an obsequious court to the people; commencing demagogues, and ending tyrants."

"Obsequious court to the people"—the eighteenth century way of saying or telling them what they want to hear—describes the career of Donald Trump in recent American history. He tells the people, especially the 25 percent who dislike or fear the Other, that is, people from other cultures, with other skin colors, that America was intended to be a country of descendants of people from Northern Europe—while George Washington made clear it wasn't; it was the refuge for all people persecuted by states and religions the world over—and that, if elected, he would make America a country totally dominated by Northern Europeans, which is impossible. Likely, many of his followers understand that it would be contrary to the wishes of our Founders and also impossible, but they accept Trump anyway because they want to and thus believe him or say they do. And by doing so, they risk the bringing on of the destruction of our democracy and opening the door to fascism and tyranny, absolutism and slavery for the American people. Americans see him for what he is—a lying, corrupt, and criminal fascist—but not enough.

The Constitution's objective is to establish, as part of government, liberty and fairness and protection for the rights of man, along with checks and balances to limit the effect of mendacity in the government. And the Founders were clear in their view of what the principal source of danger was—it was not threats from abroad. The principal threat to liberty lies within the state as explained by Alexander Hamilton, quoted at length in the *Federalist Papers No. 1*.

Jefferson and Paine held similar views about the role and mission of government, but they were different. Jefferson saw government as the entity to ensure the triumph of the rights of man and access to them for all humanity, eventually. Paine saw government more as something necessary, but not desirable, to prevent the evil present in all of mankind from blocking access of society to those rights. Society and government are different and have different origins. To quote Thomas Paine in a salient passage, "Society is produced by our wants, and government by wickedness . . . Society in every state is a blessing, but government, even in its best state, is but a necessary evil; in its worst state, an intolerable one . . ." Absolute governments are the worst states and are "the disgrace of human nature."

Alexander Hamilton said that usually the men who overthrow republics begin as domestic demagogues and end up as tyrants. America as an independent country in its first 245 years (until 2021) had not encountered a true attempt at tyranny. Whereas, Americans lived under the British king and his parliament as subjects of his empire. They, as other such colonials, experienced a long and violent abuse of power which behavior gave them the right to "inquire into the pretensions of both and equally reject the usurpations of either." America has met its first demagogue, attempting to make himself into a lifetime tyrant, in the form of Donald Trump. On top of a virtually unlimited number of serious and intolerable acts of criminality, he has likewise given the people of America cause to introduce inquiries about his intolerable acts and other destructive, un-American behavior.

The name of this would-be tyrant, dictator, despot, and unprincipled felon, again, is Donald J. Trump. Trump first brought himself to the attention of the American people in 1989 while working as an allegedly corrupt real estate manager and salesman. A terrible crime of rape and assault was visited upon a young woman, who was left on the ground near death in Central Park one evening in 1989. Five young Latino men were charged with this crime, convicted, and imprisoned for long terms. New York, at that time, no longer had the death penalty on its books.

Trump, in a lengthy advertisement in the *New York Times* the day after this horrible crime, said in strong terms that New York should reinstitute the death penalty statute, and while he did not specifically call for the five accused in this case to be executed, he said of criminals in general, "when they kill, they should be executed for their crimes." Some twenty years later, someone else confessed to the crime. His statement was found to be plausible and consistent with the evidence in the case. The five men were released, exonerated, and subsequently they concluded a financial settlement with New York City. Trump wrote another statement about the case all those years later to the effect that the five men were guilty of mugging people. When journalists asked if he would apologize for his initial advertisement, he refused and wrote his second statement instead. He maintained this position even after he was elected president in 2016.

In 2014, he publicly denounced President Barack Obama, as he was another part of the Other as an illegitimate president of the United States in that he was born in Indonesia where his mother lived for a few years—after she lived in Hawaii. President Obama's father was Nigerian, his mother was American. Obama was forced by political denunciations, by Republicans, to produce his birth certificate from the state of Hawaii to prove he was a natural-born American.

These two incidents and others established Trump as a man to be believed—and the 25 percent of the electorate that wanted to hear it and believe that Trump was such a man—when he said that America belongs to Northern Europeans and everyone else here either should be deported or remain as a second-class citizen. Trump understood this was the case from these incidents and other observations, and so he based his 2016 campaign on that idea. As Hamilton said, he was paying obsequious court to at least part of the people; he was telling them what they wanted to hear. Trump was likely correct when he said that his base support would continue to support him, even if he openly shot someone dead on Fifth Avenue. His base didn't care what he did; all they wanted were racial statements and actions by Trump. This was enough, if 20-25 percent more of the voters could be added to his base, to win. The additional votes were obtained by intimidation and death threats supplemented by Russian manipulation of the electorate by Russian posts on Facebook and Instagram and other sites so as to confuse a significant number of voters. Added to this were online ads placed elsewhere that were false as well as money contributed to the "right places." Even with all that help to Trump from the Russians and others, Hillary Clinton would have won in 2016 if Bill Clinton had been allowed a larger role in the campaign and/or Bill Clinton's remark about the importance of the Midwest had been taken seriously by her campaign organization. It just shows how vulnerable Trump is—with his 91-34 felony indictments—to a strong, intelligent, and competently run campaign.

Trump, surprisingly to himself and many others, won the 2016 presidential campaign. He lost the popular vote to Hillary by almost three million votes but won the electoral college vote, which is what matters. This was the second time in five administrations that the president was selected by a minority of voters. And a man who thought he was born to be king thought, somehow, he had been elected king. He was a horrible president. But nevertheless, he was king or pretender (in reality)—a man who wants to be king but isn't truly in line to be, as in medieval times. Further defined as a person who pretends, especially if for a dishonest purpose, he thought he should be automatically reelected. Just to mention one of his faults, when the COVID-19 pandemic arrived in 2020, for a long time he tried to ignore it, and he assured the American people it would soon go away. After tens of thousands of unnecessary deaths, he understood he had to change strategy. He was constantly on television suggesting various madman ideas on how to stop the virus, at one time suggesting that the people consume Clorox disinfectant and clean out their insides. The companies who make cleaning fluid had to publish ads urging people not to consume their product. When he lost the election (81 million votes to his 74 million votes), surprisingly, the would-be king didn't lose by 7 million votes after he declared himself an admirer, and was probably on the payroll, of the Russian President Vladimir Putin, who wants to do the US in; he also described himself as "in love" with the crazy North Korean dictator Kim Jong Un. He then organized a coup setting a huge, violent mob on course to trash the Capitol where, pursuant to the Constitution, the Congress was holding a joint session to count the electoral college votes and declare the winner, which, of course, was Joseph Biden with his 81 million popular votes. Pretender Trump ordered his vice president, rather than correctly count the votes as the Constitution instructs him to do, to fix the vote and reverse the outcome, declaring Pretender Trump the winner. To his everlasting credit and honor, Vice President Mike Pence refused to do that. Whereupon the mob was ordered to find Pence and kill him. In addition, the assault on the Capitol was accompanied by many other blatantly illegal actions that were part of the coup attempt, such as fabricating false electoral college votes and trying to insert them in the process in a number of states as well as in the final Capitol count.

The count in the Capitol on January 6 was interrupted for several hours as members of Congress ran for their lives and hid from the violent mob, protected by guards. Finally, the National Guard arrived to support the Capitol police, who were doing their best to hold the mob off, telling the mob they had to leave, many shouting that they would be back with guns next time. So, the count was resumed; Biden declared the new president— and not a king, and the republic was saved. A narrow escape from Pretender Trump. My predecessor Thomas Paine stated in *Common Sense* that King George III of England carried out "a long and violent abuse of power" in America. That he did, and the 1776 Revolution was wholly justified, as the Declaration of Independence makes clear; but alongside Pretender Trump, King George was a saint.

In late 2020, just before the election ultimately caused Pretender Trump to leave his throne, he held a celebratory party in the Rose Garden at the White House. It was a joyous group of right-wing-thinking people marking the ascension to the Supreme Court of the third of Pretender Trump's appointments to the court who, when added to the two right-wingers he had already appointed to the Court, virtually assured the overturn of the Roe v. Wade case, which established a woman's constitutional right to an abortion within certain rules. This had long been advocated prominently by the Federalist Society, a group of highly conservative lawyers, among others.

The great journalist of the *Washington Post*, Michael Gerson, wrote an article referring to Pretender Trump as the "mad king," offering to the Supreme Court Amy Coney Barrett (the fifth vote against Roe v. Wade) as the "golden apple." He told his supporters he was offering her—if his followers, particularly the Federalist

Society, would just ignore a harmless virus in their lives (COVID-19) and continue to support him, Trump—as this wonderful gift that would be theirs. If they could simply ignore the tens of thousands, becoming hundreds of thousands, of deaths from the virus. *Wouldn't we save many more lives by banning abortion?* Pretender Trump's supporters thought to themselves. Pretender Trump asked the Federalist Society for support since he delivered what they wanted—a Supreme Court committed only to the law that existed at the beginning of our country—even though our Founders clearly wanted a government including a Supreme Court that would move with the times. Pretender Trump wanted continued support from the principals of the above-mentioned far-right legal society, even though, as Gerson explained, he was a king (a "mad" one) who always despised any restraint or check on what he wants to do, a pretender who cares nothing for the rule of law. Even now, he is targeting his political enemies through fake and fantastic charges and this mad pretender would never agree to any peaceful transition from his royal place.

His offer is therefore tainted. He will give them the gifts of power that they want but only if they abandon all of their own principles and sense of honor.

Even if our Founders never encountered any human being as corrupted and unhinged as the mad king, Pretender Trump, they nevertheless had something to say about this possibility.

> "If there be a principle that ought not to be questioned within the United States, it is that every man has a right to abolish an old government and establish a new one. This principle is not only recorded in every public archive, written in every American heart, and sealed with the blood

of American martyrs, but is the only lawful tenure by which the United States hold their existence as a nation."

—James Madison, 1788

"The natural cure for an ill administration, in a popular or representative constitution, is a change of men."

—Alexander Hamilton, 1787

Pretender Trump was a habitual, pathological liar. He lied about things he had publicly admitted being lies. The *Washington Post* put a three-man team on him during his first three years and analyzed all of his speeches and other public statements. They estimated that approximately two-thirds of his statements and comments were untrue to a substantial extent. It literally was impossible to ever believe him on anything. In his fourth year, the somewhat less precise estimate was that approximately 80 percent of his public utterances were untrue.

Among many priceless comments, observations, and facts, the three-man team from the *Washington Post* (Glenn Kessler, Salvador Rizzo, and Meg Kelly) brought us the following: He repeatedly said that "U.S. Steel just announced that they are building six new steel mills"; that wasn't true. He said that, as president, "Obama gave citizenship to 2,500 Iranians during the nuclear deal talks." It didn't happen. Over and over, Trump claimed that the Uzbekistan-born man who, in 2017, was accused of killing 8 people with a pickup truck in New York had brought two dozen relatives to the United States through so-called chain migration. The actual number was zero. Not being a king by title, maybe he could be a dictator. When President Xi in China was made dictator for life, Trump expressed the thought that maybe we should try it here. From his earliest days as president, he expressed high regard for such sordid characters as Duterte in the Philippines, Putin in Russia, and Xi in China.

On May 18, 2018, Thomas Friedman warned in the *New York Times*:

> "[These institutions—free institutions in the United States—] will have to hold on for another two and a half years, and that will not be easy with a president like Trump, who was surely not 100 percent joking when he said in March of President Xi, 'President for life . . . I think it's great. Maybe we will want to give that a shot someday.'"

Of course, in order to be a dictator, especially a dictator for life, you have to value loyalty above competency and honesty. Trump certainly qualifies on this point. Michelle Goldberg of the *New York Times* wrote about this in her article, "Convictions and the Price of Trump's Delusions" on April 5, 2020:

> "Over the past three and a half years, Americans have had to accustom themselves to a numbing barrage of lies from the federal government. In one sector after another, we've seen experts systematically purged and replaced with toadying apparatchiks. The few professionals who've kept their jobs have often had to engage in degrading acts of public obeisance more common to autocracies. Public policy has zigzagged to presidential whim. Empirical reality has been subsumed to Trump's cult of personality. . . . America was once the technological envy of the world. Now doctors have had to warn the public that contrary to the president's musing in the briefing room, it is neither safe nor effective to inject disinfectant."

In his column, "Trump Should Know the Rule: Three Reichs and you're out," Dana Milbank in the *Washington Post* on May 26, 2024, pointed out how much Pretender Trump likes to copy Adolf Hitler. He hates immigrants if their culture and appearance is different from Northern Europeans, particularly those on our southern border. To denounce them, he chose language that Hitler used about the Other, particularly the Jews; they are "poisoning the blood of our country" and calling them "vermin."

And to follow this up, Janelle Bonie wrote in the *New York Times* in her article, "Trump's Taste for Tyranny," on May 26, 2024, that candidates in presidential elections make promises to the electorates, which when elected, they try to keep. Trump's promise in 2016 was to build a wall on our southern border to keep immigrants out and make the Mexicans pay, which he failed to do.

His promise this time is to round up in the United States every undocumented or questionably documented alien and promptly deport him or her. This is perhaps in the range of 20 million people, most of whom have jobs, families, pay taxes, and have been here for years—in some cases many years—being good citizens, even without formal citizenship.

Trump's proposed deportation plan, to which he is committed, would be a great crime on a level with the expulsion of the Cherokee Nation and the attack on Wounded Knee. It would rank with some of the atrocities committed by Russia and China in recent years. Twenty million people would be torn from their homes and sent to who knows where or under what conditions. These people have families, spouses, and children.

Trump, as mentioned earlier, has seemed desirous of carrying out Putin's every wish. He and Putin gave a press conference on

July 18, 2018, following the Helsinki summit meeting. Trump told the public that when he had asked Putin about US intelligence claims of massive Russian intervention in his favor during the US election of 2016, Putin had said openly and directly that it wasn't true. Trump went on to say that he believed Putin and that there was nothing to this claim of Russian intervention. He did this in front of the world press, and, with Putin sitting in a nearby chair with a slight smirk on his face, Trump overruled his own intelligence advisors in favor of Putin's account. John Brennan, former CIA Director, referred to Trump's performance as "nothing short of treasonous." One could say, I suppose, that, while Trump did not earn the title of king, he did earn the title of quisling—or maybe Mad King.

When he met with Kim Jong Un, the leader of North Korea, Trump was meeting with a declared favorite and reported to the press that Kim was a "very talented man."

And Pretender Trump clearly not only wants to establish his own royal legitimacy but his dynasty's right to rule as well. Donald Trump Jr., the heir apparent, recently said that outside of Washington, DC, the Republican Party no longer existed; it was the Trump Party or the MAGA Party, apparently a sound expression by the heir in Pretender Trump's mind.

But in every despotism or dictator-ruled state, champions rise up on behalf of liberty and truth. One such potential leader, among others, has done so in America. Her name is Liz Cheney, a conservative Republican, who gave up her promising career in Republican politics in order to defend the Republic against the ravages of Pretender Trump. She is already now an established leader. She has said recently that Trump is nothing but a "con man" and a "would-be tyrant." Trump is trying to come back from his electoral defeat in 2020 and the defeat of his attempted coup in 2021 and be elected president again, dictator for life and king. Cheney has explicitly said that if elected again this November 2024, Trump would "torch the Constitution" and its guarantee of freedom of speech, the rule of law, and the entire Bill of Rights. Cheney said in a talk in Hartford, Connecticut, reported by David Ignatius in the *Washington Post* to

> "the repeated roars of approval from the nearly 3,000 people in the audience . . . 'I will do everything I can to make sure [Trump] is never anywhere near the Oval Office again.' If he were to win, 'we'll be living in a nation that's unrecognizable, and the danger is so grave that, for the first time in my life, I will be working with every fiber of my body against the Republican nominee for president."

The Democratic nominee's victory in November is essential to save the country from potential dictatorship. We all should follow Liz Cheney's leadership and save our wonderful country and democracy from vicious, chaotic destruction. And remember John Adams's words that "Democracy never lasts long . . . There never was a democracy yet that did not commit suicide." Democracy is inherently fragile and must be vigorously defended always. Because "liberty once lost is lost forever."

John Adams, as quoted above, and others of our Founders like Benjamin Franklin—who observed in response to the question "Well, Doctor, what have we got? A republic or a monarchy?"—"A republic, if you can keep it"—believed that democracies are essentially fragile and don't last long. They inevitably seem to commit suicide. If the American people reelect Donald Trump after his many crimes and much foolishness, that will likely result in adding one more name to the list of democracies that have committed suicide. So, this country must not waver as it faces forces of the dark side in defending liberty.

And now Donald Trump has a new achievement on his record. He is the first president to be impeached twice. He is the first president to be indicted for criminal behavior. Now, he is the first ex-president to be convicted of a felony—34 of them in all.

On May 31, 2024, the *Washington Post* reported on its front page,

> "The sudden turnabout made for a dramatic end to the seven-week criminal trial that stands to define the current campaign and this entire chapter in American history, at once making Trump the first former president convicted of a crime and the first presumptive major party nominee running as a felon."

Steven Levitsky, a professor of government at Harvard, said,

> "What's notable here is that the entire Republican Party is marching in lockstep, along with right-wing media, claiming that the legal process has been weaponized, and therefore eroding public trust in a really vital institution."

And is any regret or contrition expressed by Trump? Hardly.

> "Trump attacked the judge [among other things, as a Colombian immigrant], his daughter, and finally, even the jury—ordinary anonymous New Yorkers called to perform their basic civic duty."

Following the Immunities case decided recently by the Supreme Court there have been important changes, which are that the Federal Documents case has been dismissed; the January 6 case has been suspended; and sentencing in the New York fraud case has been postponed.

In any case, no matter what happens, the point has been made: Trump is a man found guilty of 34 felonies; he is a criminal, a felon who will be representing the Republican Party or the Trump cult, whichever is now the correct name. It may be that many Americans will not want to be represented in their highest office, the country's highest magistracy, the seat where George Washington, Abraham Lincoln, Teddy Roosevelt, Franklin Roosevelt, General Dwight Eisenhower, Ronald Reagan, and many other distinguished Americans once sat, by a convicted criminal, guilty of 34 felonies, according to a jury of his peers. It could be a supreme disgrace. But time will tell; indeed, the ultimate outcome will be in the hands of the voters.

As the *Washington Post* editorial board said,

"In a way, Mr. Trump is right. Even now, his ultimate accountability—the ultimate verdict on him—may well have to arrive via a different means, the ballot box, and it will not be up to a jury of 12 but an electorate of millions to deliver it."

On the ROLE of GOVERNMENT in CIVILIZATION

FOR MORE THAN 150 THOUSAND YEARS since homo sapiens appeared on earth, the trails of large animals, whose meat permitted man's continued existence, were followed for food. In pursuing the animals for food as hunter-gatherers, man also noticed the grain that grew in many places and could be used for food as well. As the Ice Age began to come to an end about 10,000 years ago, humans began to stop pursuing the animals as they moved north with the warming climate. Gradually over maybe the next 5,000 years or so, humans began to settle in places that seemed felicitous and grow the grain themselves, making that the staple of their diet. Thus, clusters of mud-walled dwellings began to be constructed in these places, and villages—the larger ones could even be called towns of a few thousand people—began to appear. When villages attained any size at all, maybe only a few hundred people, rules were required, and someone had to enforce the rules, so kings were required. These early villagers regarded the kings as a priceless gift—order could be brought to their lives and existence could be regulated.

So, soon there followed humanity's growing problem that was not solved then, not solved over the centuries and millennia, and not solved now, as Donald J. Trump has vividly demonstrated. How should humanity govern itself? In most cases it would seem to be a form of monarchy or the near equivalent:

- by election;
- by inheritance;
- by inheritance accompanied by divine right—the assertion by the ruler that God put him there (the biggest lie by government throughout history along with all the others);
- monarchy through seizure of a neighboring state;
- monarchy by revolution against the people;
- dictatorship—by one man or by a committee like the Bolsheviks;
- absolute rule;
- limited rule, as in England in centuries past;
- rule by prominent men (and women), as in an oligarchy;
- a republic in public statements, oligarchic in practice;
- an emperor (a dictator who has conquered other states);
- a military bureaucracy;
- a real republic directly ruled by the people;
- a small segment of the people in a real republic, for example, property-owning men as in Athens or in the United States in the early decades;
- by most adults, men and women, in a democratic republic as in the United States and some other countries in the twenty-first century.

Nothing really worked. About this dilemma, Winston Churchill, the great leader of the twentieth century, said, "[D]emocracy is a worst form of Government except for all the other forms that have been tried from time to time." Some examples follow.

Again, gradually, those groups of dwellings made from mud with perhaps a thatched or otherwise constructed roof became larger and more numerous. Earliest in the Middle East, primarily in the so-called Fertile Crescent area and Egypt, but eventually everywhere, groups of towns and larger villages developed common ways of doing things—a culture. They coalesced into what could be called rudimentary states. Now their kings needed assistants, so bureaucracy of an early form slowly became sophisticated bureaucracies and aristocracies. Early on, it was necessary to develop a way of choosing kings when one died or could no longer work. The easiest way to do so was to leave the kingship in a particular family; it became hereditary until overthrown by another family. The same practice was developed and applied to early aristocracies, so hereditary rule has been part of the human condition for many thousands of years. As states grew larger and more powerful, this practice grew more and more complex, only occasionally interrupted by some means of selection by the people who were ruled by these entities called kingdoms or governments, taking many different forms. Athens in Greece is claimed to have invented democracy—direct rule by an elite segment of people; although ancient Greece was a civilization that began in relatively recent times, perhaps around 1600 BCE. The early great states such as Egypt, Syria, and the Hittite state were kingdoms coming on the scene between 900 and 3100 BCE. They grew so large and powerful that they conquered neighboring states with their armies and made these conquered states subsidiary states, thereby becoming an empire. Often the governments, like most of the kings, were hereditary and ruled by men who often had a different title—not king, but emperor, from the Latin *imperator* (commander). Rome itself developed a republic after overthrowing the king, which was ruled by a Senate—a body of prominent members, all men, who were selected by an election by their peers and whose leadership changed every year; this practice began around 509 BCE. But it was after the collapse of Greek democracy, and then the Roman republic, instituted by Caesar and his one-man rule—leader of the senate for life—about 50 BCE on through the glory days of the Roman Empire and the Dark Ages before democracy and republics were heard from again, with the exception of a few powerful states that called themselves Republics but were oligarchies in reality, ruled by a few powerful families. In the modern kingdoms, rule by women was rare and usually by a queen who had inherited the throne.

During the Middle Ages and Renaissance period, two entities carrying the name of republic became political and military powers as well as culturally significant. One of these two was the Republic of Venice, which called itself a republic but was actually an oligarchy, ruled by a group of merchants and aristocrats. The ruler was the Doge, elected for life by the Great Council of Venice and to a significant degree controlled by the Council from the time of the Council's establishment in 1142. The Doge existed continuously from 697, founded by refugees from German attacks on the collapsing Western Roman Empire. Venice was under the Byzantine Empire or Eastern Roman Empire, which survived until the fifteenth century. It controlled the Republic of Venice for several hundred years, but Venice gradually attained its independence during the Renaissance, becoming a formidable political and military state.

Florence was founded by Julius Caesar in 59 BCE, when the Roman Empire fell apart; in 846, Florence came under the ruler of Tuscany who was called the Margrave and subject to the Holy Roman Empire in the Middle Ages. Florence was ruled by about 15 aristocratic merchant families for a time. Then, the Margrave was restored for many years. In 1230, the House of Medici was established, and it became the dominant force in Florence. Florence was called a republic but in fact was an oligarchic republic led by the Medici family, intermittently. In 1434, the first ruling Medici leader was Cosimo de' Medici. It was a secular state. In 1512, Giovanni de' Medici, later Pope Leo X, reacquired Florence, intending to make Florence a religious oligarchy republic. This was resisted by Savonarola, a monk, an effective agitator who dominated this theocratic republic. He was overthrown by a different family, a group who had Savonarola hanged and returned the republic to its former status as a secular, oligarchic republic.

The Medici family did not return to power until 1512, and from 1498 until 1512, Niccolo Machiavelli was an important senior advisor to the leader of the republic. The Medici returned in 1512 and remained in control until 1527. They removed Machiavelli from power and for a time treated him quite badly because of his relationship with the previous government. In 1520, this treatment had ended, and he was asked to write a history of Florence.

The Medici were deposed a second time in 1527 during the War of the League of Cognac. In 1531, following an 11-month siege, the Medici were restored a second time by Austrian Hapsburg Emperor Charles V and Pope Clement V, who was a Medici. He arranged for his relative, Alessandro de' Medici, to be appointed Duke over the Republic of Florence in 1532, ending the republic and reforming it into a hereditary monarchy. The Medici were subsequently made grand dukes and stayed in control of Florence until 1737. But during its days as an oligarchic and religious republic, Florence founded the Renaissance period of European history, and it was perhaps during this time the artistic, cultural, political, and economic center of Europe. But, like Venice, Florence was always a republic in this oligarchic sense, based on families, not in the Athenian sense of direct rule by individuals who were property owners meeting and visiting in a large congregation.

The real republican, like Athens, or democratic form of government had always, through the centuries of recorded history, been an exceptional mode of government until the eighteenth century. Venice and Florence were examples of oligarchic republics that were prominent and important. Since the dawn of history, government had usually been authoritarian and hereditary. Rare had it been where the people ruled directly, even on a limited basis, until the 1700s, beginning with rule by prominent citizens, under a constitutional monarch; then, the American and French revolutions took place, but as centuries passed, it was the late twentieth century before broader-based direct democratic rule had flourished in various places.

Looking again at the Roman Empire after the collapse of the republic, the concept of autocratic rule returned. Julius Caesar led the return to autocratic rule as the areas conquered and ruled by Rome became—in the view of Caesar—too large to be managed by an elective, even though oligarchical in practice, regime. Caesar was succeeded by his nephew Octavian, who after the outcome of the struggle with Mark Antony and Cleopatra was determined by a large battle in the eastern part of the empire. This changed the system from a republic led by prominent men to an empire ruled by one man, ultimately by the military but not immediately. Octavian called himself Caesar Augustus and First Citizen, but not Emperor. Later rulers began to use the title Emperor, but the role of the leader of the Roman state stayed in Caesar's family for nearly 100 years, ending with Emperor Nero. Then it reverted to the strongest military man available. Initially, this was a joint rule—at least in theory—by the emperor and the senate, but the power of the senate rather soon faded away and certainly was gone when there were no more descendants of Julius Caesar wearing the purple.

But the development of the emperor's position going to the man with the strongest army led the rulers of Rome to adopt a new practice. The ruling emperor would adopt, as his son, the man he thought best to rule Rome as his successor. He would then be considered emperor designate. This system brought an extraordinary period of peace, from the 90s CE to nearly the end of the first century; during this time, Rome was a great economic and political success. Then an emperor decided to change the rule—Marcus Aurelius, thought to be the philosopher king, according to Greek philosopher Pluto, the best kind of ruler. Marcus decided to appoint his natural son to succeed him, rather than the best man. The result was catastrophe. Chaos followed, and then Rome declined into a standard military dictatorship subject to rule by the man with the biggest and best army. The emperor was not much more than the head of a large armed gang. One more system that worked for a time, but proved not to work out in the end.

The United States has always called itself a republic, even as it gradually changed from rule by the propertied classes to rule by all the people. There are a number of other states today that call themselves democracies or republics and are such, but increasingly, they are becoming more of a minority. It is of the highest importance that the United States prevail in the defense of its liberty. It already has been through many crises and preserved its democracy, and so it shall again.

Most of the kingdoms, empires, and military dictatorships, at least in the classical period of the ancient world—the Dark Ages, the Middle Ages, and the Renaissance—were authoritarian, but there were sufficient exceptions to authority to make the various regimes almost oligarchical, such as powerful provincial dukes and barons, even in the kingdom period when kings claimed they ruled by divine right, attested to by the pope.

But there was another, more severe approach to kingship, which appeared in the mid-sixteenth century, introduced by Ivan the Terrible of Russia, called the tsar. He began as an authoritarian king, supported by local princes or lords (boyars). Then midway in his reign, his wife was killed, he believed, by some of the boyars. His army, after initial successes, suffered some serious reverses. He lost control of his judgment and committed many crimes against his people, especially the boyar class. After a time, he introduced absolutist rule, in which there was only his own personal power; moreover, his decisions could not be questioned—no one had any authority, save him. He had a secret police, dressed in black, who rode black horses to support his rule. Russian tsars after him tended to follow his example.

The nineteenth century was a period, after the American and French revolutions, when the republics and democracies gradually increased in number. The American Revolution, which established the United States of America pursuant to the 1787 Constitution, and the Republic of France after a revolution, which led to excesses and a military dictatorship headed by a creative but authoritarian general, Napoleon Bonaparte. This was followed by various royal governments, revolutions, a reformist king, and a second empire with a less-authoritative Napoleon. All told, after nearly 100 years past the storming of the Bastille Prison in 1789, which touched off the original French Revolution, the French instituted a republic, which has been relatively stable ever since. Over time, the United States of America evolved from a republic to a democracy, in which the public that sustains the state is not just prominent or property-owing people as was the case in say, the Venetian republic, but literally all of the people who vote directly to select their leaders. George Washington was elected president by prominent men. Joseph Biden, the most recent president, was elected in a process where most people of voting age were eligible to cast a vote. This is still the case, and the United States remains the strongest of the world's free states, both democracies and republics. Long may it last! And may victory over its frequent enemies always be achieved.

By contrast, the tsar in Russia was overthrown in 1917 by a savage terrorist group, after an interim parliamentary democracy of less than a year, called the Bolsheviks, who introduced the Communist Party as Russia's ruling party after achieving the power to do so. It wasn't long (1922) before Joseph Stalin became the head of the party and the leader of the Soviet Union, in reality the Russian empire. He was Ivan the Terrible writ large, killing millions of innocent Russians during his reign. Contemporaneous to a degree was Adolph Hitler and the Nazi Party in Germany, which overthrew a weak republican government that replaced its king (kaiser) in Germany after the First World War. Fortunately, Germany, after the Second World War, permanently eliminated the Nazi Party and replaced it with a republic—which is actually a democracy, based on the width of voter participation—which now governs Germany. And the country is a strong supporter of democratic rights.

Unfortunately, the opposite happened in Russia, where, after an abortive attempt at democracy, Stalin and his successors were followed by another would-be Stalin—although far weaker so far—by the name of Vladimir Putin, who, unfortunately, has partnered with an unprincipled and corrupt demagogue in the United States to try to overthrow the government here and bring the United States under the influence of Putin and his dictatorship. Trump, for his own part, would like to rule America, following at least the basic principles of Russian rulers—most importantly, authoritarian leaning toward absolutist rule, supported by a secret police. A very dangerous man is Trump; fortunately, less than competent himself and surrounded by mostly sycophants—men and women like him, hired only on their subservience to him, not because of any competence or talent. He has several times stated that he will establish a dictatorship in the United States if reelected, withdraw the US from supporting NATO, and terminate support for Ukraine in its war with Russia. He would align himself closely with Vladimir Putin of Russia, whom he considers a real leader. Liz Cheney on national television in January 2024 asserted that if Trump is elected, there will never be another presidential election. She appealed to citizens of America to support their Constitution; Trump has made it clear that, if elected, he will trash it.

Our problem is that, as historian Heather Cox Richardson has written,

"On April 15 on ABC on *This Week* show host George Stephanopoulos interviewed New Hampshire's Republican Governor Chris Sununu about his switching his support from South Carolina's Nikki Haley to Trump in the primaries. 'To sum up,' Stephanopoulos said, 'you support [Trump] for president even if he's convicted in [the] classified documents (pause) case. You support him for president even though you believe he contributed to an insurrection. You support him for president even though you believe he's lying about the last election. You support him for president even if he's convicted in the Manhattan case. I just want you to say that the answer to that is yes, correct?' Sununu answered, 'Yeah, me and 51% of America.'"

Trump was indicted on 91 felony charges spanning four cases—two federal and two state (New York and Georgia). In the New York case, Trump was convicted on 34 felony charges of fraudulent behavior. In the federal classified documents case (40 felony charges), there have been obstacles placed in the arc of justice. Following the Supreme Court decision in the so-called Immunities case on the first of July 2024, which ruled that the president enjoys total immunity for all official acts while president and afterward, none for private acts, but any private act can be argued to be official while in office and some may be later. In the wake of this catastrophe, the classified documents case was dismissed, even though most of the alleged illegal actions took place after Trump left office. The federal election interference case (4 felony charges) on the attempted coup is on hold.

Sentencing in the New York case is postponed. The fourth case, in Georgia (originally 13 felony counts, but 3 were dismissed), has been disrupted by Trump partisans. Trump has been made an enormously dangerous man if elected. Under the Supreme Court's Immunities decision, Trump can, without any legal liability beyond impeachment and removal from office, order nuclear weapons to be launched at another country he doesn't like or have a political rival killed by Seal Team 6 or other military organization. Sadly but likely, Governor Sununu will still support Trump, even though Trump has been convicted by a jury of his peers in a civil fraud case and was judged guilty of 34 felonies. Obviously, by the same margin as the 1857 Dred Scott Case (6-3), which touched off the Civil War—and with some of the same motives—the present Supreme Court has taken Trump off the hook for many intolerable acts. Let's hope with respect to Sununu that the above judgment concerning Sununu will not prove to be true, but it might. Sununu's 51 percent is an overstatement; it's more like the low 40th percentile, but it still represents the Fort Sumpter in America's new civil war. It has similar issues to the first Civil War and similar importance. Indeed, some argue that it's the last great battle of the first Civil War.

CHAPTER 3

REPUBLICANS

IN MANY WAYS, the United States of America has been the greatest, most successful republic or democracy, indeed perhaps the greatest state in world history. It began as 13 British colonies in North America that wanted to be free, desired the fruits of democracy, and were committed to the view that all men (and women) were equal, and it brought, eventually, this concept of liberty and equality from coast to coast in a substantial part of North America. During this expansion, it slowly evolved from a republic to a democracy. This happened not least because of its additions of the 13th, 14th, and 15th Amendments to its Constitution of 1787 and Bill of Rights—the first ten Amendments—and through the later contributions of Abraham Lincoln, without doubt America's greatest president and a Founder of the Republican Party.

But there was one big problem that our original Founders could not solve and that was slavery. It was so ingrained in the economy of many of the states of the new republic; Washington, Adams, Hamilton, Jefferson, and Madison, perhaps our most influential Founders—including our first four presidents, covering a span of 28 years from 1789 to 1817—were forced to compromise and they hoped slavery would gradually fade away as opposed to abolishing it in 1787, much preferred by Adams and Hamilton and somewhat by Washington. The compromise was necessary to avoid a failure of the Constitution and likely civil war in 1787, so slavery was recognized in the Constitution.

But the Civil War did come nearly 75 years later, and its aim served to at least technically abolish slavery; it did, without doubt, establish at least the principles of a democratic state and its actuality by, perhaps, the year 1990.

In 1852 and through the rest of the 1850s, it appeared as if the stronger regime would be, post-1787, the slaveholding South, operating through the southern half of the Democratic Party. This party was originally founded by Thomas Jefferson as the Democratic-Republican Party, which had followers in both the South and North. But over a number of decades, the South never embraced the cause of liberty, a fundamental part of the revolution as well as the country's founding documents—the Declaration of Independence, the Constitution, and the Bill of Rights. It became an oligarchy and kept, for the most part, its governors, senators, and congressmen in place as long as it was, in a specific case, in the interest of the South. Former vice president and longtime senator John C. Calhoun was the architect of this policy. So, by 1850, the South had a grip on the Congress, the presidency to a degree, and the Supreme Court, which was in slaveholding hands by a count of six votes to three (the Supreme Court today is dominated by a similar standing vote—although this may be changing). On March 6, 1857, Chief Justice Roger B. Taney read the majority opinion of the Court, which stated that enslaved people were not citizens of the United States and therefore could not expect any protection from the federal government or the courts. From there it was but a small step to the Civil War. This situation was reversed by Abraham Lincoln's 13th, 14th, and 15th Amendments to the Constitution. African Americans were set free by the 13th, their citizenship guaranteed by the 14th, and their right to vote guaranteed by the 15th—although many challenges lay ahead.

Hamilton was the principal opposition to Jefferson; Hamilton's party was initially called the Federalist Party. It evolved into the Whig Party, taking the name of a British party.

In 1854, the Slave Power dominated Congress and Congress passed the Kansas-Nebraska Act, opening up all new territories gained after the Mexican-American War (1846-1848) to the establishment of slavery, thereby repealing the Missouri Compromise, which had been engineered by Henry Clay and had kept the peace for 30 years. Then in 1857, the Supreme Court, in the Dred Scott decision, explicitly ruled it unconstitutional for those of African descent to claim any "of the rights and privileges" enjoyed by those of European descent. At this point, one of history's greatest champions of liberty, Abraham Lincoln, rose up from the mists of the populace and of history to defend this nation.

Abraham Lincoln was a member of the Whig Party, which was unable to cope with the slavery question, and, after the passing of the Kansas-Nebraska Act in 1854, joined the new Republican Party, which was prepared to do battle with the Slave Power for "Life, Liberty, and the pursuit of Happiness" and for the country. The Republicans quickly won a number of seats in Congress. Lincoln advanced through the party through a series of magnificent speeches and gained the Republican nomination in 1860. A reform-minded Republican Party, led by President Lincoln, not only gained a majority in both houses of Congress in 1864, it gained a two-thirds majority of both houses, giving it the right to override presidential vetoes.

This last was most important as the peerless Abraham Lincoln was assassinated by a pro-South fanatic at the end of the Civil War, and Lincoln was succeeded by Andrew Johnson, a pro-slavery (albeit anti-Confederacy) right-wing Vice President, who became a horrible president. His veto of the 14th and 15th Amendments was overridden by Congress, and both became part of the Constitution by 1870. However, although Ulysses S. Grant tried to keep the Lincoln legacy alive, sadly, the most remarkable political party ever—the Republican Party—gradually and completely had its reform instincts pushed aside, and control of the party, by the 1880s, fell into the hands of corrupt Wall Street tycoons. And this left the South to again fall into the hands of an authoritarian, racist oligarchy, and the newly freed African Americans to be controlled by Jim Crow legislation and the Ku Klux Klan.

So, from the 1880s onward, the Republican Party became the party of the robber barons and the corrupt rich. The economic focus of the country was now on the industrial North. The slaveholding South was, before the Civil War, by far the richest and most powerful section of the country; now it was the poorest, as its economy remained focused on agriculture—cotton. But it was still guided by the same Calhoun principles. African Americans were no longer slaves, but they were in effect chattel slaves tied to the larger plantations or working for small farmers on smaller legal lots. They had virtually no mobility, despite the 15th Amendment guarantee; their opportunities to vote—meaningfully—were few and far between, all this being permitted by the Jim Crow legislation in the Southern States, which were totally under the control of the white establishment. And the Klan kept them in line.

But the South regained its political influence after the Republicans left the Lincoln reforms and pursued the dollar for the robber barons. Through an uneasy alliance with the Northern Democrats, which remained what it had always been, a party dominated by social issues, despite most national elections keeping the White House in the hands of the Republicans. Because of the oligarchy in the South, they could keep their representatives in place virtually indefinitely in the House and Senate and, thereby, through the seniority process, maintain control of most of the major committees of the House and Senate. The Democrats maintained this advantage to some degree even when the Republicans held the majority in Congress, with Southern Democrats staying with the Northern Democrats. This ended formally with the Nixon campaign's "Southern Strategy," when Southern Democrats began conversion to the Republican Party. The South is now almost 100 percent Republican.

There was an attempt to revive Lincoln's principles around the turn of the twentieth century by President Teddy Roosevelt and those politicians who were with him, such as Bob La Follette from Wisconsin and Henry Cabot Lodge from Massachusetts. Progress was made, but overall, much of it was only temporary. Nevertheless, the Roosevelt-Taft administration did accomplish some very important reforms, defeating a threat not too different than the one facing the country today.

During the 1890s, the robber barons pressed steadily to economic domination of the country through trusts, holding companies, and interlocking directorates of companies. The largest such trust was the Standard Oil Trust, presided over by John D. Rockefeller. For Teddy Roosevelt, the last straw was the Northern Securities Company case. In early 1901, J. P. Morgan combined two-thirds of the steel industry companies into the U.S. Steel Corporation, controlled by Morgan. The combined company was appraised at $1.4 billion, almost three times the annual budget of the US government at that time. Then, later in the year, Morgan and railroad magnates brought together the nation's principal railroad companies to form the Northern Securities Company, a holding company (a holding company exists to hold the stock of other companies to control ownership). Morgan was attempting to put the nation's steel interests as well as its railroad industry into his personal control. This type of action, developing over the previous decade or two, was concentrating economic and, as a result, political control into fewer and fewer hands. A financial oligarchy was being established, which would soon develop into a political one. The *Chicago Tribune*'s reaction to the Northern Securities matter was, "Never have interests so enormous been brought under one management." Some believed that four men then controlled the country—J. P. Morgan, Andrew Carnegie, John D. Rockefeller, and Jay Gould. Their economic dominance was, of course, mirrored in Congress.

Roosevelt was furious. He regarded this development as a direct blow to liberty and deeply un-American. He made a breakup of the trusts and the prevention of new ones a central theme of his presidency. He publicly referred to individuals that would pursue the objectives of Morgan and the others as "malefactors of great wealth." The financial abuse, engendered by the robber barons, energized the elimination of the trusts by the Roosevelt and Taft administrations. The last great breakup was the Standard Oil Trust in 1911 (becoming many companies) that was achieved by the Republicans before Taft had left office (in 1913) and before turning over complete political control of the party into corrupt Republican hands, which dominated the country during the 1921–1932 period. During this time, the Federal Reserve Board, the Treasury, the Interior Department, and the entire Harding, Coolidge, and Hoover administrations engaged in policies that led directly to the stock market crash of 1929 and the resultant Great Depression.

But Teddy Roosevelt accomplished much. He prevented, by his breakup of the trusts, the United States from being made into an oligarchy and likely, over time, a dictatorship. And he enacted three hugely important laws that became central to American life. In 1906, public attitudes toward him had changed and Roosevelt's policies had become highly popular. In that year, over the objections of the Republican Old Guard, the following three measures were passed by Congress:

- The Hepburn Act gave the federal government the power to set maximum rates for railroads;
- the Pure Food and Drugs Act made it illegal to make, sell, or transport adulterated or fraudulently labeled food or drugs;
- and the Federal Meat Inspection Act gave the federal government power to regulate and inspect factories that packed meat for shipment across state lines.

This trio of laws were watershed steps in giving the federal government power to protect citizens from the abuses of industrial capitalism.

To sum up President Roosevelt's attitude toward J. P. Morgan and his ilk, Morgan talked with Roosevelt (with the Attorney General present) after Roosevelt expressed his public opposition to the Northern Securities action and others like it. Morgan asked whether they couldn't "fix it up" if there were any problems with the Northern Securities action, as undoubtedly, Roosevelt always had. The President said, "That can't be done." The Attorney General added that "We don't want to fix it up, we want to stop it." Senator Al Beveridge of Indiana, another Republican ally of Roosevelt's, effectively said the same about Northern Securities a few years before the Northern Securities action itself, when he attacked its ways of doing business. He did so by means of expressing an opinion on a similar action. He said that each such outrage committed by business interests require "rebuke, regulation, and restraint." A good motto for all time.

Unfortunately, the Republicans didn't stay long in the Lincoln revival mode, but in 1920, captured the presidency and the Congress and promptly returned to the philosophy of the Old Guard and robber barons taking the American people right over the cliff after the Roaring Twenties spree for a few years.

For a time, the Republican Party was really down, but it began to find its way back somewhat under the highly conservative and isolationist policies of Senator Robert Taft, son of President Taft; he made a sort-of verbal pact with the Southern Democrats that the Republicans would support their racist policies in the South if they would support the Republicans, generally. This liaison began to develop, and after some 20 years, the South began to be right-wing Republican instead of Democrat, which remains the case today. This has had a profound effect on America.

But Taft failed in his last effort to achieve the Republican presidential nomination in 1952 after World War II. It appeared to be in his hands until his meeting with General Dwight Eisenhower early in 1951. Eisenhower had been asked by President Truman to leave his post as president of Columbia University and assess whether NATO, which had recently been created, was armed well enough to stop the Soviets. Ike concluded that NATO desperately needed financial support from the United States to improve and modernize itself to be able to do anything against the Soviets. He went to see Taft for support in this. A number of people previously had urged Eisenhower to enter the race for president himself in this perilous time, but Ike wasn't interested in adding politics to his career. He asked Taft for support, and Taft replied that he was opposed to the US sending money to any foreign country. Understanding that NATO had to be revived to prevent world domination by the Soviet Communist empire, Eisenhower replied that, in view of Taft's attitude, he would have to run himself. Thus began the second glory period for the former Lincoln party, which had trashed itself in 1870 as the leader of the free world and the creator of the worldwide rules-based world order. The Democratic Party played a major part in this as well. But it was Presidents Reagan and H.W. Bush that ended the Cold War by working with Soviet leader Mikhail Gorbachev; Reagan and Gorbachev set the stage for the virtually bloodless end of the Cold War by agreeing in writing at their first meeting in Geneva, Switzerland, in 1985 that "a nuclear war cannot be won and must never be fought." These three presidents—Eisenhower, Reagan and H.W. Bush—were top-tier near-great or great leaders who played such important parts in the Cold War drama and thereby gave much to their country.

Sadly, this all seems to be ended. Newt Gingrich became Speaker of the House in 1995 and pushed the conservative

Republican Party far to the right. Then Bill Buckley, the brilliant ultraconservative philosopher from Yale, made right-wing Republican politics into a religion. Donald Trump, arriving on the scene as a candidate in 2015, gradually converted the party into his personal corrupt cult, which it now is. And admission to the cult requires the supplicant to agree that the presidential election was stolen from Trump, who was running for reelection in 2020. This is against the background of President Biden actually winning that election by seven million votes—81 million versus 74 million—and the creation by Trump of a vast apparatus of fake electoral votes, organizing a violent coup attempt to stop the counting in the Capitol of the real electoral votes, and many other illegal and fraudulent acts committed by Trump and his associates to virtually try to steal the election for himself. So, in order to be a member of Trump's cult, falsely labeled as the Republican Party, someone has to agree openly to a huge, monstrous, evil lie which is nearly four years old as of 2024.

Relative to the cult leader described above, perhaps now one should look at the party or cult activity in recent times to see it as it is—a cult led by a dishonest and corrupt man. Never before in American history has any major candidate for any important office, most especially not the presidency, created such a thing.

The essence of democracy and the rock on which our Constitution rests is the peaceful transfer of power. In 2020, Donald Trump, in his effort to be reelected as president—despite an appallingly bad record of actually serving in that job— completely trashed the principle. He proved former President Barack Obama to be correct, who said in 2016 that Trump was "uniquely unqualified" to be president (doing such things as paying scant attention to the COVID pandemic in a manner to cause several hundred thousand avoidable deaths in America and then suggesting Americans cure themselves of COVID by ingesting disinfectant such as Clorox). But then failing at reelection, he put a plan in place, beginning one year or more in advance of the election, to overthrow the government and void President Biden's election—utilizing fake alternate electoral college votes and taking many other corrupt actions, as well as sending an armed mob to the Capitol to prevent Vice President Pence from counting the real electoral college votes and declaring Joe Biden president. When the vice president refused to be involved in such a scheme, Trump expressed his approval of the mob's chant to kill him. When all this failed, with Congress initially terrorized and Pence in hiding, the resistance of the Capitol police to the mob backed up after a time by the National Guard, forced Trump to call off the mob and Biden was certified as the elected president by the Senate, which the Constitution requires. Subsequent to the counting of the votes by the vice president, Trump left town, not attending the inauguration, violating one more American tradition. He then spent the next four years building his 2020 election-denying cult, basing his political career on the ONE BIG LIE principle and soon will be in place again, representing the Republican Party in the General Election in 2024—that is, if it still can be called that and not the Trump Cult, as Donald Trump Jr. suggested. Along this line, Senator Ted Cruz was interviewed on CNN on their 9:00 p.m. news show on May 22; he is a Trump supporter and, therefore, a 2020 Biden election denier and supporter of Trump's claim the election was stolen. He was explaining that he couldn't say that the 2024 election was fair in advance, so how could he say that he could support the result in advance. A preposterous position, of course. Should the Constitution have said something about all candidates being bound by the election results in federal elections if the vote was fair?

Cruz claimed that there was massive fraud in the 2020 election, although it was declared by the office in the government overseeing it to be the cleanest ever. Cruz said that an Electoral Commission should have been set up post-2020 as was done in 1877 (when the Republicans stole the election from the Democrats). Cruz should have been asked what the composition of the membership of the 1877 Electoral Commission was. It was eight Republicans and seven Democrats, and the vote was eight to seven to put the Republican candidate—who had lost the popular vote—in power. 1877 was the first time anything like this had happened. Lincoln never would have let it happen, but this was the first step of what truly was the Grand Old Party (GOP) becoming the party of corruption, and, then today, no longer a party but seemingly a cult.

By May 2024, more than Trump were declaring that the presidential candidates should be bound by the electoral vote in early November only if they, in November, thought it was fair. Senator Tim Scott (R-SC) was asked at least six times during a TV interview on May 5 about whether he would accept this November's election results. As reported in the *Washington Post* on May 8, Scott "repeatedly declined to do so, only saying he was looking forward to Trump being president again." It is, of course, crucial to our democracy that both candidates agree to a peaceful transfer of power—which neither the Republican Party nor its boss, Donald Trump, is willing to do. Again, under this circumstance, it is difficult to think of the Republican Party as an American Constitutional party.

Other examples of Republicans around the country who

refused to commit to respecting the November election have been North Dakota Governor Doug Burgum, only saying he was "looking forward to next January, when Vice President Harris certifies the election for Donald Trump." Representative Elise Stefanik (R-NY) said, in effect, she would not agree to certify the November election, saying, "We will see if this is a legal and valid election." And Representative Byron Donalds (R-Fla) "went even further—all the way to 2028. He said that if he were the sitting vice president at the time of that year's election, he would decline to certify the results 'if you have state officials who are violating the election law in their states.' In other words, he would do what Vice President Mike Pence quite properly refused to do: impose Trump's will over that of the American people," reported the *Washington Post* on May 9, 2024.

President Biden and the White House have said that the president will accept the 2024 results. His campaign has repeatedly criticized Donald Trump and his allies for trying to spread doubt about the legitimacy of elections in America. One of his aides said, "Donald Trump's last Vice President barely escaped the violent mob on January 6 and now refuses to endorse him because he understands the threat that Donald Trump poses to our democracy . . ." reported the *Washington Post* on May 8. Around the country, when voters are asked how confident they are that their votes will be counted accurately in November, two-thirds have responded they were "very" or "somewhat" confident that they would be counted accurately. That figure drops to about 45 percent when you speak only with Republicans. Michael K. Miller, a political science professor at George Washington University who studies how democracies end, emphasized to *USA Today* (May 15, 2024) the impact that election denialism has on the future of self-government in America. He stressed that "It's extremely corrosive to democracy . . . democracies have collapsed when elected leaders convince citizens they cannot trust elections."

Trump has been charged by Georgia with election interference for trying to reverse the vote against him. In Georgia, the case at its basic level is simple. Among other actions, Trump—with senior White House officials sitting beside him—called, a month or so after November 2020, Georgia Secretary of State Brad Raffensperger and demanded that he find him 11,000-plus votes to reverse the presidential outcome in Georgia. Raffensperger refused and politely said that he couldn't do that. Trump harangued him for an hour; Raffensperger continued to refuse to carry out a completely illegal order from the President of the United States and then politely hung up. In 2023, Georgia, led by the Fulton County (Atlanta) District Attorney, brought an election interference case against Trump and a number of his associates. The case has plunged into a maelstrom of political controversy as Republicans from all over the country have tried to discredit the District Attorney, who has not been free of mistakes herself, but, overall, has done an excellent job. The case continues, however.

In Arizona, ten Republican officials, headed by Rudy Giuliani, former Mayor of New York and Trump's lead election lawyer in 2020, have been charged with establishing a conspiracy based on fraud and forgery to interfere with the 2020 electoral process. That case is just beginning. Who knows? There could be others.

In addition to the Georgia election interference case cited above, Trump was charged by New York in a fraud ("hush money") case. He was also charged by the federal government in two cases—a classified documents case and an election interference case. Collectively, these four cases amounted to 91 felony charges. The federal classified documents case has been dismissed (following the Supreme Court's Immunities ruling); the federal election interference case has been suspended. Only one case has come to trial—the fraud case in New York, involving hush money allegedly illegally given to a former professional romantic partner of Trump's. The jury in the New York case has discharged its duties, finding Trump guilty of 34 felonies.

Other activities in 2024 on behalf of Trump by his supporters of an illegal nature included the following:

As the *Washington Post* reported on May 23, 2024, on page one,

> "Republican activists in at least three states where Donald Trump tried to reverse his defeat in 2020—nearly all of them under criminal indictment for casting electoral votes for him despite his loss—are poised to reprise their roles as presidential electors this year."

It is essential that Ukraine prevail in its fight against Russian aggression. To fail would be to question the long-term viability of NATO and immediately threaten the continued existence of the Baltic States. For nearly six months, the Republican Party blocked the passage of the aid bill for Ukraine and others, significantly weakening Ukraine on the battlefield. And when the logjam was finally broken and the bill passed, helping Ukraine along with Israel and Taiwan, a majority of Republicans still voted against Ukraine—an act directly damaging to US national security, an act better suited for a cult than a national party. George Will had a comment on this in the April 24, 2024 *Post* in an article titled "So, 112 Ignoble, Infantile Republicans Voted to Endanger Civilization."

> "Stoking the passion that is their excuse for pandering—the nihilism of a febrile minority in their party—a majority of House Republicans voted last Saturday to endanger civilization. Hoping to enhance their political security in their mostly safe seats, and for the infantile satisfaction of populist naughtiness (insulting a mostly fictitious 'establishment'), they voted to assure Vladimir Putin's attempt to erase a European nation."

In recent years, Governor Greg Abbott of Texas has declared that an invasion is taking place on his southern border, being carried out by the thousands of drug-cartel-controlled Mexicans attempting to cross our border. The federal government is supposed to protect the states from invasion but is not doing so for Texas at this time, he said. The Biden administration has failed to meet its obligation to defend Texas from this invasion. Texas has the right under the Constitution, therefore, to defend itself and secure the border itself. Since the Constitution was created by a compact among the states, Texas or any state can discontinue its cooperation with the federal government when it believes its rights are threatened. The governor, in this matter, is supported by 25 other Republican governors, with Abbott making 26 (there are currently 27 Republican governors). Only the Republican governor of Vermont refused to go along with this blatant assault on truth and on the Constitution.

There is no invasion; the crowds at the southern border pleading for refuge are almost entirely families and largely consist of women and children. There was no compact among the states establishing the Constitution. It was established directly by the people of the United States, not by the states, as the opening phrase of the Constitution makes clear: "We the People" are establishing this Constitution. As a result of his assertions, Governor Abbott has opposed federal agents whose job it is to process would-be immigrants on the southern border. He has mobilized the Texas National Guard to use force to enforce his declaration. Other Republican states have offered to send troops. And in doing so, South Dakota governor Kristi Noem has said that Texas and the 13 original colonies would never have signed the treaty establishing the Constitution if they had been required to give up their right to defend themselves. She apparently was unaware that when the Constitution was signed in 1787, Texas was a province of Spain. Perhaps she dropped out of school early to go into politics. Needless to say, the Supremacy Clause in the Constitution puts all border policy in the hands of the federal government, in addition to there being no compact. Abbott often says that secession is available if Texas cannot secure its rights under the Constitution, even though the Supreme Court has declared that secession is illegal and unconstitutional. During the Civil War, the Confederate states were not independent states; rather, they were illegal, rebel entities.

So, these assertions of 26 out of the current 27 Republican governors are therefore wrong; their assertions are corrupt lies, simply fashioned for political reasons to get votes in the upcoming elections. It appears that the governors didn't want Trump to get too far ahead of them in lies and corruption.

Maybe a look at some of Trump's plans if reelected could persuade some cult members to reconsider their membership. In order to round up the roughly 20 million innocent undocumented immigrants he says he will deport—he plans to deport mostly identifiable families—Trump will deploy the National Guard to ransack our cities, towns, and countryside. Maybe Putin will lend his friend and employee some Russian riot-control military and police to help.

Also, the National Guard—perhaps also with Russian military help—likely will be sent into our cities nationwide to fight violent crime. Even though the FBI says crime is declining, Trump claims, of course, the FBI is lying.

Trump says he will release all January 6 terrorists who have been convicted and are in prison.

Likely, all that he will bring into government will be election deniers so we can be confident it will be filled with slavish, incompetent Trump sycophants. This will ensure that every crazy idea the president comes up with will be carried out by his administration, causing chaos and disaster everywhere. In foreign affairs, he will cut off funding from the US to Ukraine, thereby enabling Putin's victory there, and eventually cut off America's relationship with NATO—formal withdrawal is complicated—thereby threatening all of Europe.

And rumors and speculation by potential convention staff in contemplating the likely GOP platform document for their Convention (July 15-18, 2024) included that it is likely to use language that is vague and ambiguous. That is because Pretender Trump does not want to reveal his plans too soon, as some of them are quite extreme: a nationwide abortion ban with no exceptions for rape and incest and prison terms for women who get abortions; politicizing the civil service; a ten percent across the board tariff; the right of parents to force children, their gay children, into conversion therapy; and a ban on gay marriage. And there could be plans to terminate Social Security and Medicare, as well as authority to force Ukraine into a territorial settlement with Russia to go along with plans to end US military and financial aid to that country. In addition, he will plan revenge and retribution to include arresting President Biden for treason and the jailing of Liz Cheney and others because all of them are guilty of treason.

The *Washington Post*, in its lead editorial on May 23, 2024, asserted,

"Of the four criminal cases pending against former president Donald Trump, the one currently being tried in a New York criminal court involves both the least serious charges against him and the most legally debatable. But whatever verdict—if any—results from the proceedings, they have already provided a damning indictment of the Republican Party over which the defendant, the soon-to-be official GOP presidential nominee, holds sway . . . the New York case and the GOP hierarchy's reaction to it are points on the continuum in which excusing little or midsize ethical violations leads to excusing bigger ones."

CHAPTER 4

AMERICA'S ROLE
and the FUTURE

So, WHAT SHOULD AMERICA DO about all this? What is our interest here? How can we advance our situation, strengthen our democracy, enhance our nation, and fulfill our obligations, both to ourselves and to the international community? To begin, we have an obligation to ourselves and to our friends to do a good job of keeping order in the world.

First, someone has to be the world's policeman. In the immediate past, for the last 75 years, it has been America. We need to maintain that worldwide rule-based order is to the benefit of all mankind. To be sure, we have been opposed by fascists, communists, jihadists, and fanatical terrorists since the beginning. We have beaten them all and we will continue beating them. Few people want to see the streets of the world patrolled by Russians carrying AK-47s or Chinese doing face-identity surveillance while bearing guns. There is no other real game in town as possible overseers of world order, there are only fascists, communists, terrorists and second-rate assorted dictators. That's why—or one important reason why—we have to win against the fascists etc., both at home and abroad, to enable us to play our proper role.

America is the richest, strongest country in the world and maybe ever. The United States is, by a considerable margin, the world's largest economy. And there are a number of reasons, but one important one is that it is the best home in the world for new starts, new ideas becoming successful companies, the dot-com center of the world, the least regulation and the most vigor to develop new ideas. Using the World Bank numbers, the US GDP in 2023 was 53 percent greater than China's and twice that of Japan and Germany combined. And when one combines the economic impact of America and that of these two close allies, Japan and Germany, the result is impressive. Add most of the rest of NATO and it is world dominating. More powerful by a significant margin than China and Russia. Russia isn't even in the top ten.

With respect to military power, no one else is on the same playing field as the US; America has, effectively, a very substantial military force counting active duty, National Guard, and active reserves and spends annually around $700 billion on its military. This ensures the availability of the highest-quality technology for the armed forces. But this very high level of spending represents only about 3.5 percent of GDP. Also, America has a substantial and sophisticated nuclear weapon force.

Therefore, America should not be pushed around by anyone. The only weakness is the appalling, counterproductive, almost un-American politics played by the Republican right wing. This, of course, is the main subject of this book. The party (if it still can be called that) leader has engaged in almost limitless criminal behavior and has very poor judgment. All of this is weakening for the country. His performance, as noted above, after he did a press conference following a meeting with the Russian president in Helsinki in 2018, in the view of former CIA Director Brennan, was "nothing short of treasonous." This is very divisive for America; some observers believe we are more divided today than at any time since the Civil War. This could well be true if Trump is reelected; there may never be another presidential election. The glorious Republic that we have had for so long would be no more. Without question, as some believe, if Trump is reelected, the result would be devastating damage to our society, our culture, the American way of life, and everything we hold dear. The pall hanging over our country will persist, and since Donald Trump appears to be beholden to and under the control of Vladimir Putin, we might someday not be free—Russian soldiers as policemen in America in some places.

Trump, on July 13, 2024, was involved in a shooting incident at a rally by a 20-year-old registered Republican. A bullet nicked Trump's ear and killed an attendee sitting in the viewing stand behind him. The gunman was killed by a Secret Service sniper. No one knows what effect this incident will have, but some are advancing the idea that Trump is a martyr. But national catastrophe may not happen. The right wing, fascism, and Donald Trump may in the end not happen as actual leaders of our country. The tip of the sun of freedom and peace can be seen on the horizon, supported by increasing bipartisanship.

David Leonhardt wrote on the front page of the *New York Times* on May 19, 2024, and presented ample evidence that this was so.

He said that the deeply polarized state of American politics may be the most-discussed subject in American politics today.

"The Republican Party has moved to the right by many measures, and the Democratic Party has moved to the left. Each party sees the other as an existential threat." One result for this polarization is the fact that nothing can get done in Washington; there is just constant gridlock. But if this is indeed true, the last four years are exceedingly difficult to explain. The last four years, since the last year of Trump during the peak of COVID, bipartisanship began and then accelerated the next three years.

During the COVID pandemic, Democrats and Republicans in Congress came together to try to do something about the horrible situation. They recognized the need—both parties did—to pass emergency legislation to try and contain the pandemic. Under President Biden, the two parties passed bipartisan majority bills on many subjects. Republicans and Democrats during the last three years have passed much major legislation with solid bipartisan majorities on infrastructure, semiconductor chips, veterans' health, gun violence, the Postal Service, the aviation system, same-sex marriage, anti-Asian hate crimes, and the electoral process. It is amazing, given what has gone on before for decades. It's as though FDR and LBJ jumped out of the closet, waved a magic wand, and disappeared. On trade policy, the Biden administration has largely kept the Trump administration's major initiatives and expanded some of them. These years have been arguably the most productive period of Washington bipartisanship in decades.

And the trend is continuing. Congress has passed several major pieces of legislation in the past few years. In addition, quite recently, it passed foreign aid bills for several allies and a forced TikTok sale. These recent bills were debated for months in the Congress, primarily in the House, and the final vote in the House was indeed impressive:

House

Ukraine Aid

	Democrats	Republicans
Yes	210	101
No		112

Israel Aid

	Democrats	Republicans
Yes	173	193
No	37	21

Taiwan Aid

	Democrats	Republicans
Yes	207	178
No		34

TikTok Sale

	Democrats	Republicans
Yes	174	186
No	33	25

Senate

Infrastructure bill

	Democrats	Republicans	Independent
Yes	48	19	2
No		30	

CHIPS and Science Act

	Democrats	Republicans	Independent
Yes	46	17	1
No		32	1

Then, to top it all off:

Block Motion to Remove Mike Johnson as Speaker

	Democrats	Republicans
Yes	163	196
No	32	11

After the votes on the substantive issues were completed in the House, a group of far-right members tried to fire Mike Johnson as Republican Speaker for voting with the Democrats and not blocking the TikTok part of the four items of legislation in the omnibus bill. The Democrats joined in support of the Republican Speaker with a very strong majority vote to save his job. "There is no precedent for House members of one party to rescue a speaker from the other," says Leonhardt.

All this is very encouraging for the future.

One reason for this development is that neoliberal economics policy has not worked out so well. This policy was based on the market economy triumphing everywhere and not the government. The new policy that these members are making accepts an important role for government. It is more like FDR and Eisenhower than Reagan. The neoliberalism policy just hasn't been effective—except for the very rich. For everyone except the affluent, the economy and salaries and wages have been growing slowly. It's not been a success; the new centrism is a response to this development and recognizes that the market economy and the government must work together.

Then there is the international competition. As Senator Collins (R-ME) said, "China is a unifying force" for America. You bet it is, and the TikTok votes show that. We are coming to realize that we are being confronted by a new Cold War experience by China, Russia, and Iran, accompanied by substate groups like Hamas and the Houthis. The rise of artificial intelligence capability in Russia threatens us the way Sputnik did during the Cold War. Anxiety about this situation made the CHIPS and Science Act possible. Pennsylvania Democratic Senator John Fetterman is quoted by David Leonhardt as follows:

> "We are most able to come together when we acknowledge the risks we have to the American way of life. Whose side are you on—democracy or Putin, Hamas and China?"

So, there's hope. Again, as David Leonhardt says,

> "For decades, Washington pursued a set of policies that many voters disliked . . . as polarized as the country is, its two political parties are at least trying to respond to that reality, and they have found an unexpected amount of common ground."

This new positive trend was forced upon Trump in his last year by his Congress trying to stop the COVID pandemic. It was continued during the Biden administration and will be continued by his successor. Trump, if reelected, based on his own statements, will not continue the policy of bipartisanship. To vote for Trump at this exceedingly dangerous yet hopeful time would be a supreme act of suicidal folly.

Very important for both parties as well as for independents—we need a strong, moderate, right-of-center party; we need a strong, moderate, left-of-center party; and we need a strong, moderate, independent sector. We don't need cults or false MAGAs. We all must come together and support our Constitution and Bill of Rights, and we must live by the principles of our Declaration of Independence. Many Americans over the years have fought and some died to protect our right—every American of both great parties, of all religions and ethnic groups and cultural backgrounds—to unite. That's what George Washington wanted after he successfully won the war for our independence, which permitted our glorious Constitution. And remember that patriots believe, as the great Senator Arthur Vandenberg, Republican of Michigan, said while Chairman of the Senate Foreign Relations Committee in the late 1940s—as the Soviet Union threatened— "Politics stop at the water's edge."

So, if I may address all Americans, if you do one civic thing this year, one activity—if you are eligible to vote—make sure that you vote in November. Nothing is healthier to our democracy than the largest voter turnout possible.

And, finally, we must continue working together in a bipartisan spirit as we have in the Congress in recent years, as described above and have in the incumbent administration and others have in civic action. This is the time when America most needs bipartisan policies pursued and put in place, as the understanding is spreading in the Congress, in the government, and in the nation as to how important that is.

God bless America!!

www.ingramcontent.com/pod-product-compliance
Lightning Source LLC
Chambersburg PA
CBHW031424250726

48656CB00002B/820